Purity of Aim:
The Book Jacket Designs
of Alvin Lustig

BY NED DREW

AND PAUL STERNBERGER

T0338935

ALVIN

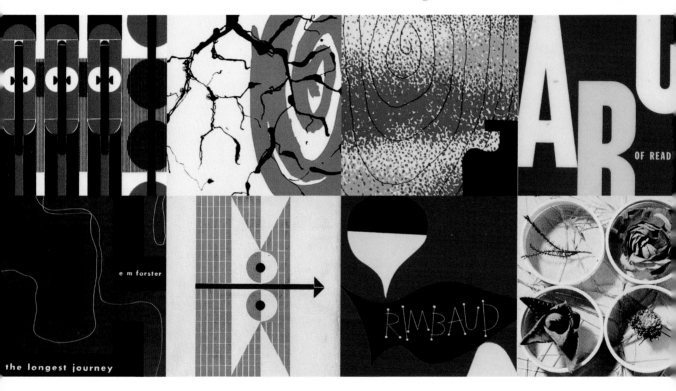

e m forster

the longest journey

RIMBAUD

AR

OF READ

LUSTIG

Purity of Aim:
The Book Jacket Designs
of Alvin Lustig

BY NED DREW

AND PAUL STERNBERGER

GRAPHIC DESIGN ARCHIVES

CHAPBOOK SERIES: FOUR

RIT

CARY GRAPHIC ARTS PRESS

2010

Purity of Aim:
The Book Jacket Designs
of Alvin Lustig

BY NED DREW
AND PAUL STERNBERGER

GRAPHIC DESIGN ARCHIVES
CHAPBOOK SERIES: FOUR

RIT
CARY GRAPHIC ARTS PRESS
90 Lomb Memorial Drive
Rochester, New York 14623-5604
http://ritpress.rit.edu

FRONT AND BACK COVER: *Portrait of Lustig, 1949,* Photograph by Jeff Moses

ISBN 978-1-933360-48-5 Printed in USA

Library of Congress Cataloging-in-Publication Data
Drew, Ned.
  Purity of aim: the book jacket designs of Alvin Lustig/by Ned Drew
and Paul Sternberger.
    p. cm.–(Graphic design archives chapbook series; 4)
  Includes bibliographical references.
  ISBN 978-1-933360-48-5 (alk. paper)
  1. Lustig, Alvin, 1915–1955–Criticism and interpretation.
  2. Book covers–United States–Design.
  3. Lustig, Alvin, 1915–1955. II. Sternberger, Paul Spencer, 1966–III. Title.
    NC973.8.L87D74 2010
    741.6'4092–dc22
        2010028428

Alvin Lustig

From the article
"Graphic Design," *Design*,
Special Issue:
Black Mountain College
April 1946

The basic difference
between the graphic designer
and the painter or sculptor
is his search for the 'public'
rather than the 'private' symbol.
His aim is to clarify and
open the channels of communication
rather than limit or even
obscure them, which is too often
the preoccupation of
those only dealing with the personal…
It is the tragic split between
the public and private experience
that makes both
our society and our art
fragmentary and incomplete.

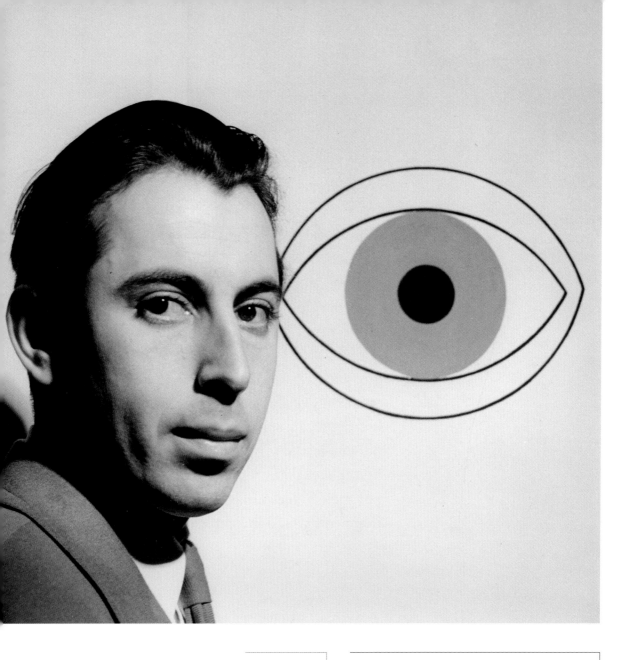

Purity of Aim:
The Book Jacket Designs
of Alvin Lustig

BY NED DREW AND PAUL STERNBERGER

1 Alvin Lustig
"Contemporary Book Design,"
in Holland Roberts Melson Jr., ed.,
The Collected Writings of Alvin Lustig
(New Haven, Connecticut:
Holland Roberts Melson Jr., 1958) 45–46.
Repr. from *Design Quarterly* 31, 1954, 2–6.

Look Magazine Offices
New York, NY 1944–1945
Photograph by Maya Deren

Alvin Lustig was among the most driven and conceptually rigorous American designers of the twentieth century. Determined to redefine the role of both the designer and design itself, Lustig gravitated toward the challenge of reconciling polarities– art and design; creativity and commerce; the spiritual and the practical; instinct and logic; the avant-garde and the traditional. While Lustig's design projects delved far beyond the realm of graphic design into fields such as architecture, and interior and industrial design, his book covers are perhaps the most eloquent articulations of his vision for design in contemporary society.

Lustig saw the book as one of the most challenging media in which to engage "the esthetic and technical changes of the twentieth century."[1] In tandem with Lustig's extensive writing on design and its place within contemporary culture, his book covers reveal the complexities of his career. They offer insights into his design theory and process, and they manifest intricacies of form and meaning that would help shape the education of generations of designers. Lustig's opportunity to use the book cover as a vehicle of bold graphic experimentation and innovation was provided by James Laughlin, founder and publisher of New Directions Books. In a collaboration that flourished through the 1940s until Lustig's early death in 1955, Laughlin and Lustig prodded, cajoled, and quibbled their way through a virtually unprecedented partnership between publisher and designer.

2 Jane Fiske Mitarachi, "The Lustig Portfolio, '53," *Interiors*, June 1953, 90.

3 Lustig, "Personal Notes on Design," *AIGA Journal* 3, no. 4, ca. 1951, 16–17.

A Fresh Eye

Born in Denver on February 8, 1915, Lustig moved early in his childhood to Los Angeles, where his father began working as a distributor for Warner Brothers. In his teenage years, Lustig's interests included magic, and though he managed to find venues to perform, he recalled spending more time on the posters announcing his engagements than on the magic itself.[2] A high school art teacher, Aimee Bourdieu, introduced Lustig to modern art and design, and the material struck a chord within him that would help shape the trajectory of his design philosophy. "An enlightened teacher, to the scorn of her fellow instructors," reported Lustig, "showed her students modern painting, sculpture and architecture, with a liberal sprinkling of European posters. Something happened. This art hit a fresh eye, unencumbered by any ideas of what art was or should be, and found an immediate sympathetic response."[3] As one might expect, Lustig's recollections of seminal events of his early years underscore themes that would guide his experimentation in design: design had the capacity to be truly effectual; the roles and interrelationships of art and design were worthy of serious contemplation; and the rationality and utility of design could be reconciled with the immediacy of instinctual response.

Remarkably, in 1933, Lustig landed a job straight out of high school as art director for *Westways* magazine, published by the Automobile Club of Southern California. But after a few months on the job, Lustig quit to continue his design education at Los Angeles Junior College, and then at the Art Center School in downtown Los Angeles the following year. Lustig's quest for education would characterize his entire career.

4 "Alvin Lustig: Biographical Notes," ca. 1950,
Alvin Lustig Collection CSC 014,
Graphic Design Archive,
Melbert B. Cary Jr. Graphic Arts Collection,
Rochester Institute of Technology, hereafter
referred to as Lustig Collection, RIT.

5 Many useful biographic details about Lustig
are provided in Steven Heller's "Down the
Pigeonhole," *Print*, January/February 2004,
76–83, 120–21.

He was never complacent or even satisfied with his present state of accomplishment, but rather he continually pushed to refine his style and expand his oeuvre, always demanding formal rigor and conceptual depth. One biographer noted that, as a young man, "he rarely stuck with any routine plan of study longer than three months at a time. Instead, he chose his own way which consisted of intensive reading, research, analysis, and experiment in various fields of design and graphic art."[4] Education in design at that point tended toward the more practical–techniques of printing and such–but Lustig was very self-motivated and sought out the creators of work that impressed him, who might offer more theoretical bases for design. For instance, Lustig contacted architect Richard Neutra whose residential architecture had caught his attention. Neutra seems to have been equally impressed by the precocious young man, giving him access to his library.[5] Lustig savored this sort of opportunity because the kind of rigorous design education he craved was not available at the time. Throughout his life, Lustig was a prodigious reader in a broad spectrum of subjects, and he stressed the need for design libraries, archives and journals as he helped shape design education in America at midcentury.

When Lustig saw an opportunity to study with a designer known for his seriousness of purpose and consistency of vision, he pursued it. In 1936 he began an apprenticeship with Frank Lloyd Wright at Taliesin East in Wisconsin. However, Lustig's expectations for the apprenticeship were not met. The somewhat willful young designer seems to have been rubbed the wrong way by Wright from the beginning. Lustig's wife and collaborator, Elaine Lustig Cohen, whom he married in 1948, recalled an anecdote that Lustig relayed to her later in his career.

6 Elaine Lustig Cohen
  "Alvin Lustig Remembered" (videorecording)
  Rochester Institute of Technology, 1989.

When Alvin arrived he was put into a guest room. Wright wasn't there… There was a blue vase in front of a blue wall, and a white vase in front of a white wall, and as soon as Alvin got into that room, he put the white vase in front of the blue wall and the blue in front of the white. Wright came back. He came in to see this new student, and without saying a word, he switched vases.[6]

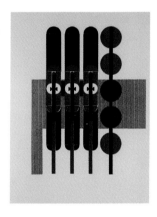

Alfred Young Fisher
The Ghost in the Underblows
The Ward Ritchie Press
1940

As trite as it may seem, the story offers insight into how Lustig thought of his own character and design aesthetic: he presented himself as resolute in his beliefs and dedicated to balancing seemingly opposing forces. Lustig persevered at Taliesin for three months until he could stand it no longer, explaining his departure to Wright in a letter he left behind.

While he reported being miserable and disenchanted at Taliesin, Lustig did learn some valuable lessons from Wright. Not just an architect, Wright was interested in all fields of design, including furniture, fabrics and graphics. Lustig, too, would argue quite adamantly that a true designer was multidisciplinary. Wright perceived himself as an outsider, and his convictions and confidence led him to become a self-reliant designer and thinker. Lustig shared these traits as well. In fact, it was after his stay at Taliesin that Lustig truly began to define his place as a designer.

Aldous Huxley
Words and Their Meanings
The Ward Ritchie Press
1940

Carl Rakosi
Selected Poems
New Directions
1941

Upon returning to Los Angeles, Lustig started experimenting with decorative type elements, creating geometric patterns and architectonic abstractions reminiscent of Wright's style of decorative detail. Word of Lustig's experiments made it to printer and publisher Ward Ritchie, who hired Lustig to design books and gave him a studio space. Ritchie had Lustig design limited edition, letterpress-printed publications, such as Alfred Young Fisher's *Ghost in the Underblows* and Aldous Huxley's *Words and Their Meanings*. In these early cover designs, Lustig struck a delicate balance of discipline and playfulness. Reminiscent of Wright's decorative style, the arrangements of elements in *Ghost in the Underblows* incorporated clusters of geometric shapes hovering above rigid, linear forms, creating a highly structured yet dynamic composition of pattern and color. In *Words and Their Meanings*, Lustig made a stark juxtaposition of the author's signature, isolated for greater effect, and an abstract configuration of shapes, referring to the inherent complexities found in systems of writing and their organizational syntax.

Lustig's early Wright-influenced work helps illustrate the young designer's journey towards maturity. From early on, Lustig's creative process included searching for avant-garde modes of expression, and Wright's work inspired Lustig to experiment and play with form in order to create dynamic, complex compositions. However, this early work often seems merely decorative, lacking the emotive and conceptual connections that mark Lustig's later, more sophisticated work. At some point, Lustig must have realized that this style had run its course, and that it was limited in its ability to communicate a conceptual connection to books he was designing. He would soon begin to develop a sense of individuality and visual sophistication that would become a key component in the covers he designed in the coming years.

By Sheer Force of Form and Color

Lustig's great opportunity to make his mark as a designer came in 1939 when Jacob Zeitlin, a Los Angeles bookstore owner, introduced him to publisher James Laughlin. Three years earlier, with the encouragement of Ezra Pound, Laughlin had founded New Directions Books while he was still an undergraduate at Harvard. Laughlin was devoted to promoting cutting-edge poetry and literature, and he would publish both new and resurrected modern classics, collaborating and cavorting with some of the century's most influential literary and artistic characters.[7] Able to infuse his small press with money his family had made in the steel and iron industry, Laughlin's first commitment was to literary merit; unlike large commercial presses, he could afford to have profit be less of a priority.[8] Nonetheless, Laughlin did want to sell books, and he understood that the design of his books could help establish a unique place for New Directions in the marketplace and at the same time create visual analogs for the avant-garde work he was publishing. Unremarkable covers, such as the pre-Lustig edition of New Directions' *In the American Grain*, reveal that Laughlin needed a designer to make his publications look as cutting-edge as they were.

7 See Barbara Epler and Daniel Javitch, eds.,
*The Way it Wasn't:
From the Files of James Laughlin*
(New York: New Directions, 2006).

8 Mel Gussow, "James Laughlin,
Publisher With Bold Taste, Dies at 83,"
New York Times, November 14, 1997.
Linda Kuehl, "Talk With James Laughlin:
New and Old Directions,"
New York Times, February 25, 1973.
Donald Hall, "James Laughlin of
New Directions,"
New York Times Book Review,
August 23, 1981.

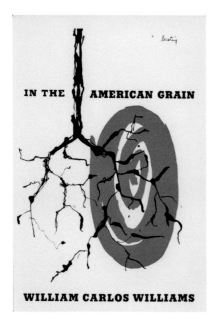

William Carlos Williams
In the American Grain
New Directions
1939

In Lustig's cover for a reprint of the book, he broke away from the more traditional, symmetrical approach to book cover design, treating it instead as a small painting and allowing the typography to act as a supporting element, framing the images. Lustig created a conceptual assemblage of abstract elements while playing against the viewer's expectations of typography as a focal point. He used the abstracted root forms to draw the viewer into the composition, encouraging an attempt to decipher the meaning of the symbols at play. Lustig's simplified spiraling circles contrasted with the roots thrusting in disparate directions. Lustig allowed the viewer's eye to work its way back out to the text only after it had engaged the image.

As Lustig and Laughlin became acquainted, the two must have recognized within each other a sense of uncompromising principles and a tenacious drive to make a mark on contemporary society. Laughlin recalled that he was drawn to the designer not only because of his unique experiments with type, but also because of an intriguing "unshy quietness of speech and gesture which is sometimes the outward mark of inner power."[9] The two would work together for the rest of Lustig's life, even when they resided on opposite ends of the country. The correspondence between Lustig and Laughlin reveals a spectrum of moods, from frequent wrangling about money, to poking fun at each other, to dense philosophical ruminations.

9 James Laughlin,
    "The Designs of Alvin Lustig,"
    Publishers Weekly, November 5, 1949, 2005.

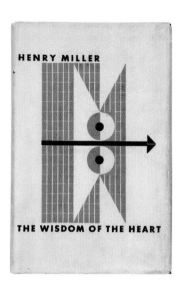

Henry Miller
The Wisdom of the Heart
New Directions
1941

10 Laughlin's definitions of his series
were somewhat fluid, and his dating of
publications was somewhat incomplete.
He developed distinct aesthetics for
each series, but books of a particular style
were not always labeled by the publisher as
part of that series. The best resource for
dating New Directions publications is
John A. Harrison, Rebecca Newth and
Anne Marie Candido, *Published for
James Laughlin: A New Directions List of
Publications, 1936–1997* (Fayetteville,
Arkansas: Will Hall Books, 2008).

Lustig's first cover for Laughlin was for a collection of
Henry Miller's essays, *The Wisdom of the Heart*. With this cover
design, Lustig continued his experiments with decorative type
elements but also bridged his early, more formal work and his
later conceptual projects. While still evoking Wright's decorative
style, Lustig began to establish a dialog of meaning between
elements, creating a visual tension that could serve as a metaphor
for themes suggested by the title of the book—conflicts between
the analytical mind and the emotional heart. Lustig incorporated
large triangular shapes to guide the viewer's eye toward the center
in contrast to the outward push of the red arrow squeezed
between the circular forms. He used color to amplify the sense of
tension, juxtaposing the fiery, passionate red with the cool blue
of the underlying grid structure.

Lustig also designed simple graphic systems for New Directions
such as the covers for the Makers of Modern Literature series,
each of which included the same simplified image of a
hand holding a pen, rendered in a different color scheme.
The collaboration between Lustig and Laughlin truly blossomed
with the New Classics series for New Directions.[10] It is with
this series that Lustig began to define his own design voice.
Lustig's covers for the intimately sized (7¼" x 5") New Classics
books mixed a vast array of experimental design elements.
Simple, dynamic compositions were brought to life through
contrasting colors, forms and scale. Lustig played hard-edged
abstract shapes against calligraphic, semi-representational
drawings. He juxtaposed hand-rendered lettering with typefaces
such as Franklin Gothic, Garamond, Bodoni and Futura. Often
limited by budget to two-color palettes, Lustig chose colors that
could be vibrant and aggressive, or muted and reserved.

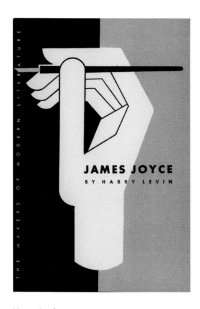

Harry Levin
James Joyce: A Critical Introduction
New Directions
1941

In the New Classics series, a simplified or abstracted image often played a dominant role, while typography functioned as a subtler complementary element that helped create a hierarchical composition. Lustig often made visual and conceptual connections by creating subtle formal relationships between type and image, trying to preserve what he would call "the potency of both form and idea."[11] In covers for books such as Arthur Rimbaud's *A Season in Hell*, Nathanael West's *The Day of the Locust*, Henri Alain-Fournier's *The Wanderer* and Henry James's *The Spoils of Poynton*, Lustig generated letter forms to mimic the character of the illustrations. In James Joyce's *Exiles*, the cover's thin, spread out letters and the delicate, organic, white abstract lines help to evoke a sense of displacement. In Rimbaud's *Illuminations*, the title and author's name echo the formal qualities of fire. While type is subservient to image in some New Classics covers, Lustig also implemented the idea of type as image. This approach is evident in the covers of Ezra Pound's *ABC of Reading*, F. Scott Fitzgerald's *The Great Gatsby*, and Nathanael West's *Miss Lonelyhearts*, where the text itself is the primary compositional element, foreshadowing Lustig's later, purely typographic work.

11 Lustig, "Formal Values in Trademark Design," in *Collected Writings*, 55–60.

12 C. F. O. Clarke
   "Alvin Lustig: Cover Designs."
   Graphis 23, 1948, 242–44.

13 Lustig, "Notes for PW on Jackets," n.d.,
   in Elaine Lustig Cohen Papers concerning
   Alvin Lustig, Smithsonian Archives of
   American Art, Washington, D. C., n. p.

Through these experiments in the New Classics series, Lustig developed a progressive visual language that could serve as an analogy for the content of the book itself. "In the jacket designed for *The Spoils of Poynton*," wrote critic C. F. O. Clarke in 1948,

> Lustig has admirably captured the spirit and style of Henry James. The criss-cross of red threads endlessly intertwined epitomizes the way in which the author builds up his theme from the tireless annotation of psychological fragments. Evelyn Waugh's entertaining yet pitiless dissection of the relations between a sophisticated modern couple in a *Handful of Dust* is suggested by Lustig's design with an astringency equaling the author's. In these as in all Lustig's jackets the approach is indirect, but through its sincerity and compression has more imaginative power than direct illustration could achieve.[12]

Lustig explained that his intentions for the New Classics series "was to establish for each book a quickly grasped, abstract symbol of its contents, that would by sheer force of form and color, attract and inform the eye." Such a symbol, he continued, "is a matter of distillation, a reduction of the book to its simplest terms of mood or idea. This spirit of the book cannot be expressed by naturalistic representation of episodes or by any preconceived formal approach, but can only develop naturally from its own nature."[13]

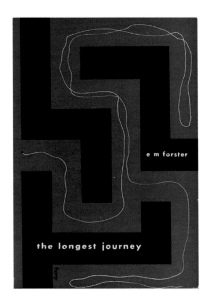

E. M. Forster
The Longest Journey
New Directions
1943

In compositions such as his cover for E. M. Forster's *The Longest Journey*, Lustig distilled symbolic systems with abstracted forms. Here, he built an asymmetrical yet balanced maze-like structure in which the blue areas defined an allusive space confined by heavy black shapes. Lustig articulated the concept of a journey through delicate, hand-drawn lines. These lines, faint and uncertain, suggest a route while also conjuring associations with confusion and indecision. Jules Langsner, a Los Angeles art critic, recognized Lustig's modernist distillation of form that aimed for more than mere functionalism:

> Lustig strives for vital compression of line and form, compression that balances a maximum weight with effortless poise. By the use of subtle color relationships on linear inventiveness, Lustig's compression provokes our interest in addition to satisfying our functional needs… In Lustig's deftly elegant compression we sense the beginnings of a disciplined ornament that yet possesses lyrical and psychological overtones.[14]

14 Jules Langsner
   "Alvin Lustig," ca. 1950.
   Lustig Collection, RIT.

15 Laughlin, "Preface,"
*Bookjackets by Alvin Lustig for
New Directions Books* (New York:
Gotham Book Mart Press, 1947), n. p.

16 Laughlin, "Designs of Alvin Lustig,"
2005−7.

17 Laughlin, "Preface,"
Bookjackets by Alvin Lustig.

The New Classics series is remarkable in its variety and complexity, in its dynamic tensions and poetic contrasts. There is neither a systematic set of formal rules nor any one uniform visual style that defines the series as a series. Yet as a whole, the series seems steadfastly consistent and cohesive. The aesthetic spirit of the covers unquestioningly binds them together, as Lustig intended. "The jackets," he explained, "were always planned for maximum visual effectiveness when displayed together, as well as when shown singly against the confused background of the average bookstore."[15] Lustig's approach met Laughlin's enthusiastic approval, in both philosophical and practical terms. "Lustig's revolutionary jackets for New Directions," Laughlin wrote, "set a distinctive style which has come to symbolize in physical terms the desired isolation of our editorial program from that of the great commercial houses. And the jackets have more than paid their way… Our New Classics Series' sales tripled after Lustig jackets were adopted."[16] High sales were more than welcome, but Laughlin felt that he first and foremost had a mission to serve an audience, a society, through literature:

> It is perhaps not a very good thing that people
> should buy books by eye. In fact, it's a very bad thing.
> People should buy books for their literary merit.
> But since I have never published a book which I didn't
> consider a serious literary work–and never intend to–
> I have had no bad conscience about using Lustig to
> increase sales. His beautiful designs are helping to make
> a mass audience aware of high quality reading.[17]

Lustig would take that argument further, insisting that they were also making a mass audience aware of high quality design.

Arthur Rimbaud
A Season in Hell
New Directions
1945

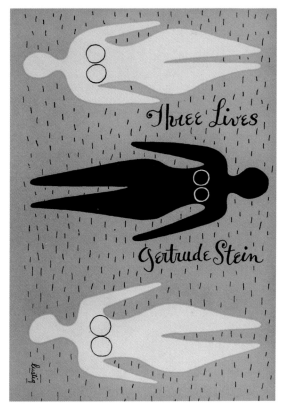

Gertrude Stein
Three Lives
New Directions
1946

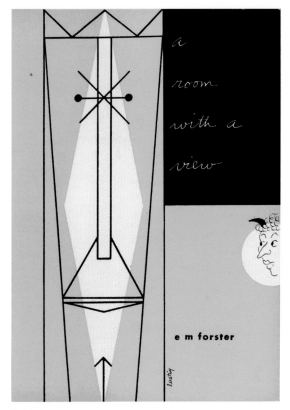

E. M. Forster
A Room with a View
New Directions
1943

Henry James
The Spoils of Poynton
New Directions
1943

Gustave Flaubert
Three Tales
New Directions
1944

Evelyn Waugh
A Handful of Dust
New Directions
1945

F. Scott Fitzgerald
The Great Gatsby
New Directions
1945

Franz Kafka
Amerika
New Directions
1946

Djuna Barnes
Nightwood
New Directions
1946

Kenneth Patchen
Selected Poems
New Directions
1946

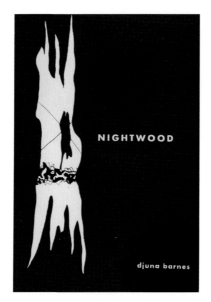 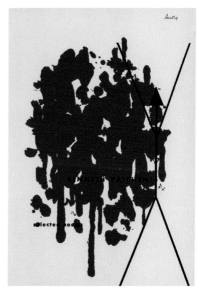

James Joyce
Exiles
New Directions
1945

Arthur Rimbaud
Prose Poems
from the Illuminations
New Directions
1946

Nathanael West
Miss Lonelyhearts
New Directions
1946

Henri Alain-Fournier
The Wanderer
New Directions
1946

Charles Baudelaire
Flowers of Evil
New Directions
1946

D. H. Lawrence
The Man Who Died
New Directions
1947

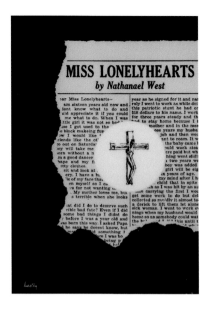

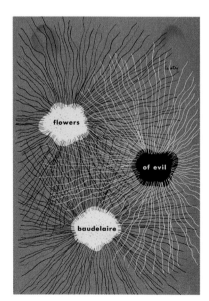
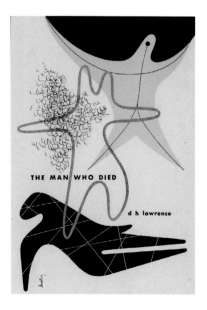

D. H. Lawrence
Selected Poems
New Directions
1947

Kay Boyle
Monday Night
New Directions
1947

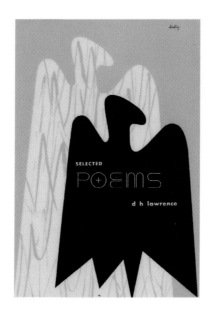 

William Carlos Williams
Selected Poems
New Directions
1949

Tennessee Williams
The Glass Menagerie
New Directions
1949

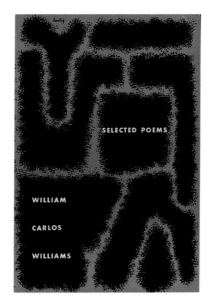 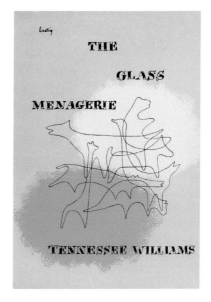

Carson McCullers
Reflections in a Golden Eye
New Directions
1950

Wilfred Owen
Poems
New Directions
1949

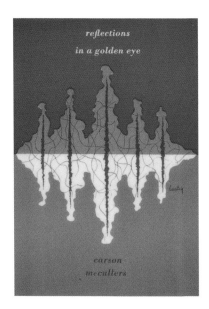
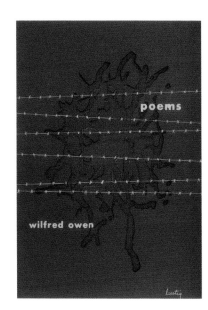

William Carlos Williams
Paterson
New Directions
1948

Stephane Mallarme
Poems
New Directions
1946

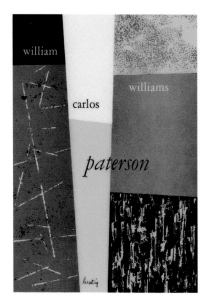
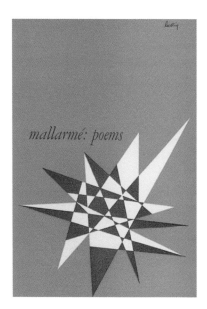

Nathanael West
The Last Day of the Locust
New Directions
1950

Madame de Lafayette
The Princess of Cleves
New Directions
1951

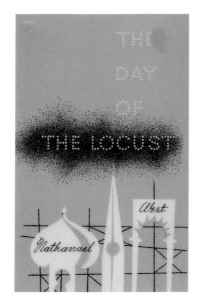

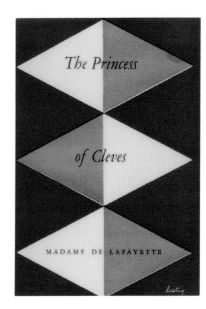

Muriel Rukeyser
Selected Poems
New Directions
1951

Joseph Conrad
Under Western Eyes
New Directions
1951

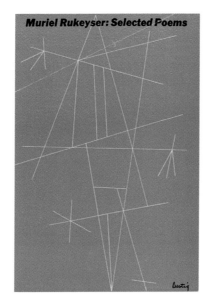

Hermann Hesse
Siddhartha
New Directions
1951

Jean-Paul Sartre
Nausea
New Directions
1952

Federico Garcia Lorca
Selected Poems
New Directions
1955

The Responsibility of a Designer to his Society

As he designed the New Classics series for New Directions over the course of the 1940s, Lustig did not simply experiment to find his own style, but began to form his philosophy of design and its place in the modern world. In response to a draft of an article that Laughlin was writing for *Graphis* about Lustig, the designer made a number of points that underscored his sense of purpose as a designer. He asked Laughlin to make sure not to treat him "as another graphic designer like Rand and McKnight Kauffer, etc." Lustig went on to explain that he acknowledged an affinity to their work, but felt he had wider and deeper aims, creating not only "symbols, but the things they are supposed to signify."[18] This graphic realm, in which form and meaning were reconciled, was a key concern for Lustig, and he went to great lengths to try to define truly effective design, design that had the power to change society. To Lustig, design in any form was "always related to human needs, both individual and social." [19]

Building upon earlier design movements and stylistic innovations of modern art, Lustig was committed to creating objects that transcended the mundane and elevated the everyday into something unique, edifying and socially constructive. Lustig's ideal designer could truly contribute to contemporary culture by "synthesizing the needs of man with the nature of materials, fusing the beauty of the fine arts with the utility of the practical arts. Herein lies the responsibility of a designer to his society."[20]

18 Lustig to Laughlin, January 9, 1948. Unless otherwise noted, letters between Lustig and Laughlin are from New Directions Publishing Corp. Records (MS Am 2077.1039) Houghton Library, Harvard University.

19 Colin Forbes, "Alvin Lustig: Design," *Advertising Review*, Autumn 1954, 71. Forbes to Lustig, November 23, 1954 Smithsonian Archives of American Art.

20 Lustig, in "Alvin Lustig... A Young Man of the West," ca. 1946. Lustig Collection, RIT.

Indeed, Lustig felt that design, treated thoughtfully, could make a significant impact on contemporary society, and that it was the designer's role to strive to make that impact. Lustig's high moral standards for the designer would lead friends like Arthur Cohen, the co-founder of Noonday Press, to identify Lustig as "one of the strictest moralists that I have ever encountered. He really thought that design was virtue."[21] To today's observer, Lustig's lofty aims may seem like musty, even naïve utopianism, but his convictions seem to have been genuine and played a significant role in his innovations as a designer.[22]

Just as he recognized that society and its needs were in flux, Lustig's own values and opinions shifted as he reflected on his own life, professional and personal. In 1948, he extolled the promise of America as a venue for a true re-conceptualization of design, yet in 1949, he drafted three pages of notes about his desire to emigrate to Israel:

> America has been quite kind to me and has allowed me the opportunity to follow my interests with a reasonable amount of recognition and reward. Yet it seems unable to supply the one missing ingredient, the sense of belonging to an integrated and cohesive community that is able to plan and direct its growth and future, with intelligence and without fear.[23]

21 Arthur Cohen, "Alvin Lustig Remembered."

22 Lustig's concept of the genuine social obligations of the designer was tied to his sense of the gravity of his own historical moment. Throughout his writings he made reference to broad forces affecting society, from the clash of ideologies of World War II to the growing tensions of the Cold War. As he considered these momentous changes around him, he worried less about political stances or individual events than how the designer could adjust both work and attitude to meet the needs of a society in flux. As the nuclear age commenced, he brooded, "If I seem to place a heavy mantle of responsibility on the shoulders of those who are really only expected to make nice shapes and colors, it is because history demands it. Every act that allows productive facilities to serve only itself, contributes inevitably to the threat of destruction that already looms on the horizon." (Lustig, in "Alvin Lustig… A Young Man of the West," 5). See also Lustig, "Personal Notes on Design, and "Design and the Idea," *Western Advertising*, June 1943.

23 Lustig, notes re: desire to work in Israel, n.d. [1949], Lustig Collection, RIT. Lustig to Laughlin, January 9, 1948.

24 In response to a suggestion that Christian Science might offer help with his gravely worsening diabetes in 1954, Lustig related having attended a Christian Science Church from the ages of 15–18, but having abandoned it because its teachings did not reveal the "basic creative and vital polarity that must exist between negative and positive forces, in order that true life and creation may exist." (Lustig to Estelle Laverne, December 30, 1954, Elaine Lustig Cohen Papers, Smithsonian Archives of American Art). Ward Ritchie, with whom Lustig had worked in the late 1930s, recalled, "During the time he was with me, we had many long and serious discussions, sometimes about intimate details of his life, but more often about his philosophy. He had discovered Jesus and strongly felt at that time that he might be the Messiah and could save the world." (Ward Ritchie to Elaine Lustig Cohen, Lustig Collection, RIT). David W. Davies also recounted this zealous Christian phase, based on Ritchie's accounts. (David W. Davies, "The Graphic Art of Alvin Lustig," 1984, Lustig Collection, RIT).

25 Laughlin, "In Memoriam: Alvin Lustig," Eulogy, 1955. Lustig Collection, RIT.

26 Laughlin, "The Book Jackets of Alvin Lustig," *Print* 10, no. 5 (October/November), 1956, 54.

27 Lustig to Laughlin, ca. early 1940s.

His flirtation with the idea of making his professional mark in the newly-founded Jewish homeland of Israel is also evidence of Lustig's personal investigations of religion. Throughout his life he seems to have explored widely in search of the proper religious fit for his approach to life and work.[24] Ultimately, personal belief and professional responsibility were perceived as inseparable in Lustig. In his eulogy for Lustig, Laughlin wrote,

> Alvin did not practise any of the formal religions, but he was, I always felt, a profoundly religious person. He always seemed directly concerned with the essences of life. His theories of art went beyond technique to a wider concept of the way in which art could enrich our lives and give the pattern of society some meaning. I never knew anyone who had a more highly developed ethical sense.[25]

The Tragic Split between the Public and Private

Lustig's ethical sense compelled him to embrace the struggle to balance creative production and social function. After Lustig died, Laughlin lamented, "I often wish that Lustig had chosen to be a painter. It is sad to think that so many of his designs must live in hiding on the sides of books on shelves. I would like to have his beautiful Mallarmé crystal or his Nightwood abstraction on my living room wall."[26] But to Lustig, being an artist would have been too easy—he felt he had social responsibilities that only design could engage. "The problem," Lustig reflected, "is how to proceed with aims such as mine, to avoid both the mockery of gestures without authority or authority gained with the loss of purity of aim. If I was simply an artist or could believe that salvation for our time is outside of the realm of social reality, then the problem would be simple and quickly solved."[27]

**Artwork for Tennessee Williams'
Camino Real**
Collage on painted board
Courtesy of New Directions Publishing Corp.
1953

As Lustig grappled with the ethical responsibilities of the designer, he concluded that, in order to achieve "a mature industrial culture," the designer was faced with the challenge of breaking down barriers between "fine" and "applied" arts and thus setting the stage for a marriage of "art and life."[28] In fact, this reconciliation of design and fine art was central to Lustig's definition of truly effective design. As one might expect of a high-minded graphic designer, Lustig condemned design's frequent "descent into hackdom and servility,"[29] where designers favored style over substance or mindlessly catered to the prosaic demands of the client. He was irritated by designers who used a formal vocabulary without understanding the syntax or the theoretical basis of design. But Lustig was also critical of "the world of personal vision occupied by the 'artist,'" where creative innovation and formal discovery failed to make a larger social impact.[30] To the spiritually inquisitive Lustig, the quest for personal expression in art was an essential element of human experience. Yet he understood that isolated creative expression could fall short of meeting the needs of contemporary society. "The basic difference between the graphic designer and the painter or sculptor," explained Lustig,

> is his search for the 'public' rather than the 'private' symbol. His aim is to clarify and open the channels of communication rather than limit or even obscure them, which is too often the preoccupation of those only dealing with the personal… It is the tragic split between the public and private experience that makes both our society and our art fragmentary and incomplete.[31]

Throughout his career, Lustig grappled with this challenge of imbuing design with the cultural significance of art, while at the same time taking advantage of design's large audience.

28 Lustig, fellowship application draft, ca. 1950, Elaine Lustig Cohen Papers concerning Alvin Lustig, Smithsonian Archives of American Art.

29 Lustig to Laughlin, January 9, 1948.

30 Ibid.

31 Lustig, "Graphic Design," *Design. Special Issue: Black Mountain College*, April 1946, n.p.

Tennessee Williams
Camino Real
New Directions
1953

32 Georgine Oeri, "Alvin Lustig."
Graphis, 1954, 324.

33 Laughlin, "Designs of Alvin Lustig," 2006;
Laughlin, "Book Jackets of Alvin Lustig," 54.

34 Lustig reported that a section of a
Clement Greenberg article on contemporary
American painting "comes closest to a
statement that I might embrace as a declaration
of personal aims." (Lustig to Laughlin, ca.
1947.) In the segment to which Lustig refers,
Greenberg stated, "The art of no country
can live and perpetuate itself exclusively
on spasmodic feeling, high spirits and infinite
subdivision of sensibility. A substantial art
requires balance and enough thought to
put it in accord with the most advanced of the
world obtaining at the time." Art should
"take off from where the most advanced
theory stops."(Clement Greenberg,
"The Present Prospectus on American
Painting and Sculpture," in John O'Brian, ed.,
*Clement Greenberg: The Collected Essays
and Criticism, Volume 2: Arrogant Purpose,
1945–1949* [Chicago: University of
Chicago Press, 1988], 167. Repr. from Horizon,
October, 1947).

35 Lustig to Harry Ford at Alfred A. Knopf
(proposal for a book on design), July 8, 1955,
Lustig Collection, RIT.

36 Lustig, Alvin.
"Designing a Process of Teaching,"
in *The Collected Writings of Alvin Lustig*.
New Haven: Holland R. Melson Jr., 1958, 21.

37 Ibid.

Lustig was determined to create an intersection between functional everyday objects and expressive, rarified and insular objects of high art. He was said to have been "fascinated by all the astonishing contemporary efforts to find forms that are really *ours*."[32] But as fascinated as he was with these forms, techniques and styles of modern art, he was dedicated to making them beneficial on a broad level, bringing art, as Laughlin put it, "out of the museums into our homes and offices, closer to everything we use and see."[33]

Lustig identified experimental modern painting as a realm of research making advances that could find real world application through design. Theory had to be put into practice, an opinion he found echoed in the essays of critics like Clement Greenberg.[34] To Lustig it was a two-way street–art needed design as much as design needed art. "The artist will only find salvation," wrote Lustig, "through some vital connection with the industrial process despite the dangers of depersonalization and mechanization that are inherent within it."[35] Painters such as Picasso, Matisse, and Miró, according to Lustig, evolved "great private symbols" that "are now waiting to be projected onto a public level."[36] Compared to the next generation of painters, design, in Lustig's estimation, had a better chance of taking on this task of truly affecting society:

> "I have a feeling it [contemporary painting] is just reheating bits that have been left on the stove by Picasso, Miró, and Matisse; whereas the designer is able to use these things, or even ransack them… I am able to take research of this sort and transform it in such a way that I can never be accused of imitation."[37]

Henry James
The Aspern Papers and The Europeans
New Directions
1950

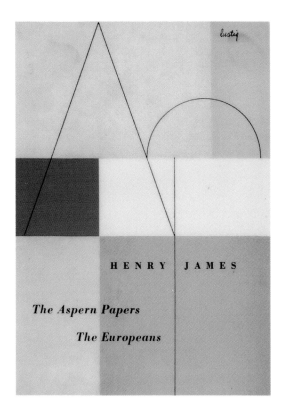

38 Langsner, "Alvin Lustig," 2.

39 Claire Imrie, "Alvin Lustig: A Versatile Designer in the Visual Arts," *American Artist*, November 1952, 32.

While a cover such as the one Lustig designed for Henry James's *The Aspern Papers and The Europeans*, with its disciplined geometric composition and subtle shifts in earthy tones, may have been reminiscent of El Lissitzky or Kandinsky, Lustig adapted their visual language to make it his own. By the mid-twentieth century, critics had identified Lustig as one who believed "it is possible to bridge the gap between the private vision and the public audience without corrupting the vision or palliating the audience."[38] And Lustig was said to frequently stress "human values and the synthesizing role of the designer–the influence that can bring technology and human feelings into relationship."[39]

40 Lustig, "Personal Notes on Design," 16. Lustig realized that the seeds of his own design philosophy had been sown by the high school art teacher who introduced him to modern art and architecture as well as Modernist design. (Lustig, "Designing, a Process of Teaching.")

41 Elaine Lustig Cohen, in discussion with the authors, June 12, 2008; Doug Clouse and Rita Jules, *Alvin Lustig, American Modernist 1915–1955*, exhibition catalog (New York: Bard Graduate Center for Studies in the Decorative Arts, 2007), 15–16; Lustig to Laughlin, ca. 1947; Hubert Crehan to Alvin Lustig, April 22, 1952 in Elaine Lustig Cohen Papers concerning Alvin Lustig, Smithsonian Archives of American Art, Washington, D.C.

Despite the fact that (or perhaps because) early in his life, Lustig had never been "exposed to any of the great symbols of European civilization except by second hand reproductions," he made it a point to be engaged with the world of fine art.[40] Lustig designed for important art galleries, such as the Los Angeles Stendahl Art Galleries, dealers in Pre-Columbian and tribal art. Also in Los Angeles, Lustig befriended patron/collectors Walter and Louise Arensberg, who owned an extensive body of work by Marcel Duchamp and various American modernists and surrealists. He was also acquainted with dealer/collector Galka Scheyer, whose holdings included works by Wassily Kandinsky, Paul Klee, Kurt Schwitters, Ernst Kirchner, El Lissitzky, László Moholy-Nagy, and many other seminal European modern artists. Lustig found personal parallels in the criticism of Clement Greenberg and his calls for art that put theory into practice. Lustig corresponded with painter/critic Hubert Crehan about groundbreaking artists such as Clyfford Still, and he knew Mark Rothko through the Stable Gallery in New York. Lustig's own library included books on the Bauhaus, Pablo Picasso, Klee, Joan Miró, and volumes from the Wittenborn Documents of Modern Art series that included books by Moholy-Nagy and Kandinsky, with covers by Paul Rand.[41]

42 Lustig to Laughlin, January 9, 1948.

43 Lustig, "Personal Notes on Design," 17.

To Lustig, the great advantage of art was its ability to speak to and from a human level, and modern art's increasing focus on immediate and intuitive expression seemed to offer clues as to how to bring true social utility to the workaday world of design. He saw the new languages of art as a springboard to create something more socially useful through design, as he put it, "synthesizing and projecting these formal discoveries into a conscious reality shared on a broad level. In other words, culture instead of 'art.'"[42] In design he saw the opportunity to take the personal expression associated with the realm of art and marry it with a communal visual language produced through design. Often visceral, emotive and abstract, Lustig's book cover designs drew their inspiration from the avant-garde art movements of the day, as well as tribal and non-Western art. In Lustig's designs, one can find compositions echoing the biomorphic shapes of Calder, Miró and Gorky, the glyph-like forms of Klee, the early work of Gottlieb and Pollock, and the fields of abstract color of Still and Rothko.

As easy as it is to find stylistic similarities between his designs and movements in modern art, Lustig's engagement with modern art was not simply an integration of art styles into design, but rather it was the integration of the creative processes of art into design. Because design could be deadened by functionality, rationality, and utility, he tried to incorporate art's instinctual and spontaneous aspects into his design process. He saw modern art's strength in its encouragement of the viewer "to 'see' freshly, unencumbered by preconceived verbal, literary or moral ideas."[43] In art, the visceral visual response preceded the rational explanation, and Lustig believed the nurturing of instinctive response could be a key to developing a process of design.

44 Lustig, "Personal Notes on Design," 16.

45 Ibid., 17.

46 Lustig to Laughlin, n.d. [1948]
   Elaine Lustig Cohen,
   discussion, 2007–08.

"Rather than present an elaborate and carefully worked out theory," explained Lustig, "I would reverse the process and try to track down the instinctive, the quite often unconscious development that leads one later to feel that such a theory is necessary."[44] By embracing the processes of art, designers could develop the unique vision of the artist and put it in service of a large audience. "As instinctive decisions slowly develop," Lustig theorized, " a system of response and action develops that makes you a specific individual with your own concept of reality. You will find delight where another finds ugliness. You will see order where another sees chaos. You will see clarity and elegance where another sees only barrenness and sterility."[45]

The Still Undefined Nature of the Designer

A cornerstone of Lustig's view of the social responsibilities of the designer was the notion that the designer should embrace a wide spectrum of disciplines. While in retrospect his most consistent and noteworthy achievements were within the field of graphic design, Lustig aspired to a much wider design practice. In fact, he encouraged friends and colleagues to think of him as more than just a graphic designer. For instance, he wrote to Laughlin about a description the publisher had written,

> I would appreciate a little stronger emphasis somewhere on my other activities of architecture, fabric design… industrial design, etc. The wide non-specialized character of my work is the idea that I am pushing everywhere I can as too many people still think of me only as a graphic designer. Of course I realize the greatest volume of my work has been graphic but I am seeking to change that balance.[46]

47 Lustig, *Collected Writings*, 1–7.
   Repr. from *Interiors*, September 1946.

48 Philip Johnson, "Introduction,"
   Collected Writings, 10.

49 Lustig moved to New York in 1944 and
   worked for two years as visual research editor
   for *Look* magazine and art director for
   Look's staff magazine, *Staff*. Lustig left *Look*
   in 1946 and returned to Los Angeles.

A designer, to Lustig, was a practitioner in many fields, an integrator of disciplines that transcended individual vocation to create something new with much more social impact. "The words graphic designer, architect, or industrial designer," wrote Lustig, "stick in my throat, giving me a sense of limitation, of specialization within the specialty, of a relationship to society and form itself that is unsatisfactory and incomplete. This inadequate set of terms to describe an active life reveals only partially the still undefined nature of the designer."[47] To an observer like Philip Johnson, Lustig's attempts to break free of stifling categories within design were the basis of his historical importance: "I think that as a book designer there might have been others we could consider to be in the same category as Alvin Lustig. But no one expressed as he did the joining together of the arts of design in a public way."[48]

Lustig did have a fair amount of success incorporating into his oeuvre projects in architecture, interior design, industrial design, fabric design, and package design. His endeavors outside graphic design included Los Angeles collaborations with architect Sam Reisbord to design the Beverly Carlton Hotel and the Beverly Landau apartment building. Lustig also designed a school and community center for the Labor Zionist Movement. Often his own living and work spaces became laboratories for his experiments in interior and furniture design, and, in addition, he had important commissions for interiors such as *Look* magazine's New York offices and the Reporter Publications offices in the Empire State Building. He also designed the personal apartment of William Segal, the publisher of Reporter Publications.[49]

Helicopter Design
Roteron Company
1944

50 For a succinct discussion of Lustig's
broad range of design projects,
see Clouse and Jules, *Alvin Lustig,
American Modernist*. See also Steven Heller,
"Down the Pigeonhole," 76–83; 120–21.

His retail environments and graphic systems included two 1947 Beverly Hills clothing stores, Monte Factor and Sheela's, as well as signage for Northland Center, a shopping mall near Detroit designed by architect Victor Gruen in 1954. Lustig's forays into industrial design included an upholstered molded plywood chair that was exhibited at the Museum of Modern Art in 1950, several innovative custom lighting fixtures, and the body of a prototype for a single-occupant helicopter.[50] Lustig even designed an exhibition of his own work that opened in late 1949 at New York's A-D Gallery, an exhibition space known for its commitment to graphic design. For the next two years, the show traveled to more than a half dozen venues across the country.

51 Lustig to Laughlin, n.d.
[late 1941 or early 1942]. Lustig wrote
to Laughlin about becoming "quite friendly
with Charles Eames" in the early 1940s,
and Elaine Lustig Cohen recalled traveling
to Pacific Palisades on weekends in 1948–49
to see the construction progress on the
Eames's Case Study house. She also told of
spending evenings with Charles Eames
and his wife Ray. As similar as their
aesthetics and broad mission may have been,
Elaine Lustig Cohen's recollection of
these evenings hinted at differences in the
designers' temperaments and professional
demeanors. Elaine remembered Alvin being
somewhat irritated that Charles brought his
slides to these social evenings. The Eames's
collection of thousands of slides was both
a means of inspiration and of self-promotion.
Lustig appears to have been less comfortable
with this sort of self-promotion–his style
was more contemplative and introspective.

52 Lustig, "Designing, a Process of Teaching,"
23. As early as 1942, Lustig was expressing
admiration for Eames's innovations.
He wrote to Laughlin, "Are you coming
in to L.A.? Suggest you wait about
two weeks as Charles Eames will be back
in town to show you an extremely ingenious
way of preforming plywood furniture in
mass production very cheaply."
(Lustig to Laughlin, n.d. [early 1942]).

Lustig's dedication to practicing a broad spectrum of design suggests an affinity to Charles and Ray Eames, who shared Lustig's interest in incorporating a range of visual languages from a variety of sources. The Eameses did in fact have a similar approach to design: they saw it as a larger pursuit, stretching beyond the borders of traditional disciplines such as architecture, furniture, interior and graphic design. Lustig and the Eameses shared a philosophy of design for a higher social good; they sought inspiration from a broad range of sources; and they took the opportunity to exchange ideas as the two couples socialized in Los Angeles.[51] Lustig saw Charles Eames as a model designer who integrated different fields of design and art, blurring the distinctions between art, graphic design, industrial design, and architecture. Lustig wrote,

> Some of the greatest examples of pure design today have been the various chairs that Charles Eames has produced. These have been produced with the greatest respect for material, the greatest respect for the technical process, the greatest respect for everything that he as a human being has been able to absorb about form and about the meaning form-relationship provides. He has brought this together with an intensity that can only be called pure. That kind of purity is still rare in design. Anything that is done without secondary considerations can be called pure.[52]

53 Lustig to Laughlin, n.d.
[late 1941 or early 1942].

54 Lustig to Laughlin, n.d. [1942].
After Lustig left, Ray Eames
stepped in to design several covers,
as did Herbert Matter, Charles Kratka,
Fred Usher and John Follis.
(John and Marilyn Neuhart, *Eames Design*
[New York: Harry N. Abrams, 1989],
30–31, 38–39, 44–45, 86–87).

The closest professional affiliation between Lustig and the Eameses was with the magazine *California Arts & Architecture,* published by a close friend of the Eameses, John Entenza. Appointed art director of the magazine, Lustig reconceived the magazine's cover and designed two subsequent covers. As he reported to Laughlin, Lustig was excited by the promise of "complete freedom as to form and with some possibility of suggestions editorially," at what he considered to be one of "the most potentially important magazines being published."[53] The covers for *California Arts & Architecture* have a similar look and feel to the covers Lustig designed for New Directions. Both the magazine and the book covers have European avant-garde influences, experimental applications of photography and photomontage, and illustrations inspired by modern art. They also share typographic similarities such as the use of Futura Extra Bold in a secondary typographic level. Unfortunately, Lustig's delight with *California Arts & Architecture* was short-lived; he left the magazine after clashing with the equally strong-willed Entenza.[54]

We Are Going to Have a Nice Long Talk
As frustrating as his association with Entenza had been, Lustig was fortunate to have an amazingly constructive and mutually respectful collaboration with Laughlin. Lustig used Laughlin as a sounding board for his philosophical introspection about design, and appeared comfortable explaining his design concepts to Laughlin. Laughlin seems to have truly appreciated the thoughtfulness of Lustig's designs, and while he was willing to express displeasure or to suggest changes to Lustig's covers, he would often capitulate to Lustig if the designer was unwavering about his concept.

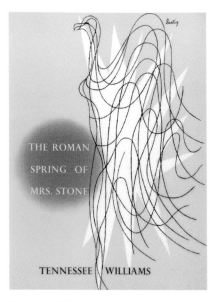

Tennessee Williams
The Roman Springs of Mrs. Stone
New Directions
1950

55 Laughlin to Lustig, April 17, 1950.

56 Letters between Laughlin and Lustig, March–May 1950.

57 Laughlin to Lustig, February 5, 1951.

In a series of letters about Tennessee Williams's *The Roman Spring of Mrs. Stone*, which New Directions published in 1950, Laughlin lobbied for the most economically-motivated cover design features, asking that the gestural scribble of a bird be shifted to allow larger type and thus better in-store exposure. Yet, while he badgered Lustig (successfully) over design features that might improve the title's visibility, he acknowledged that the sketches for the cover were "visually extremely effective."[55] Beyond his faith in Lustig's designs, Laughlin also valued Lustig's editorial input on the manuscript, even trying to convince Williams to accept Lustig's suggestion of an alternate title: *Cold Sun.*[56]

When authors insisted on having input on the covers of their New Directions books, Laughlin could be adamant in his support of Lustig. For instance, in the process of preparing Muriel Rukeyser's *Selected Poems* for its 1951 New Classics printing, Laughlin reported that

> Rukeyser is raising bloody hell about her jacket.
> I myself think it is very beautiful and am giving her back as good as she hands out. She wants to have another design made, and I have told her flatly that nothing can appear in the New Classics Series unless it is a Lustig, and that if she wants to have you do something else, she will have to pay for it. I think this will hold her. She is a bloody nuisance. It is a beautiful jacket.[57]

Always working to explain his designs and educate his client, Lustig was also self-reflective about the ever-shifting directions of his design theory and aesthetic. Along with his sketches for the cover of Henry James's *The Aspern Papers & The Europeans*, Lustig sent Laughlin a letter to explain them.

Ezra Pound
Selected Poems
New Directions
1949

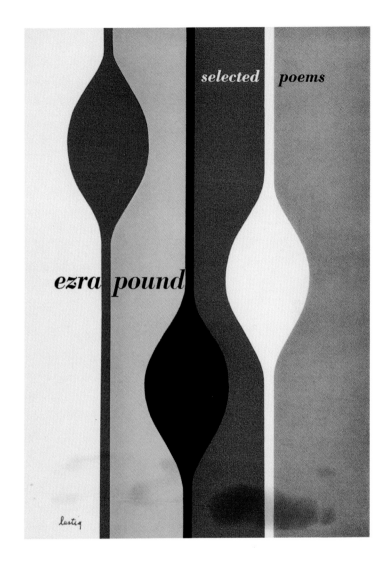

It is done in just black and brown, the tones being ben-days of each. Rather than use any associative symbols, I have made a design which although very 'modern' is related in character to the subtle, precise, and muted nature of James' writing. I find a growing tendency on my part to return to an architectural, formal approach rather than the associative symbols. Relationships to the content in this case becomes [sic] more a reflection of the mental climate of the book, rather than an effort to deal with specific allusions.[58]

This move from the symbolic toward the abstract in the New Classics series may even have been influenced, albeit indirectly, by Laughlin. In 1949, Lustig and Laughlin struggled to agree on an acceptable cover for Ezra Pound's *Selected Poems*, leading Lustig to confess to Laughlin, "I was not kidding on the Pound. Frankly I feel that Pound is a rather sinister character and the cover probably projects that too much for your taste. I will send you a 'beautiful' and serene one free of all nasty symbolism. By God you had better like this one as it will be number four on dear old Ezra. He ain't worth it, poet or not."[59] Laughlin replied, sympathetic to Lustig, but also in defense of his old mentor, "Don't get discouraged about Pound and don't imagine for a moment that he is sinister. He is one of the sweetest people alive and it is just too bad that he had to go crazy. He is also the greatest poet of his age, next to Eliot, and nothing is too good for him."[60] Laughlin wrote again the following day relating that he found the shapes of the cover interesting, but found the colors "rather deadly and dull." He went on to explain, "Perhaps if this were done in more attractive colors, it would be all right. There is a predigious [sic] gayety and exuberance and joie de vivre in Pound which I don't feel that you have caught at all."[61]

58 Lustig to Laughlin, February 6, 1950.

59 Lustig to Laughlin, January 27, 1949.

60 Laughlin to Lustig, February 1, 1949.

61 Laughlin to Lustig, February 2, 1949.

Ezra Pound
ABC of Reading
New Directions
1951

Lustig's reponse to Laughlin's comments is telling. He did try to adapt the design to a livelier palette, but came to the conclusion that the earlier version was the strongest. And Lustig was not afraid to abide by his principles, even at risk of offending his client. He wrote Laughlin,

> Now settle back, we are going to have a nice long talk about the Pound design. When I sent it to you I felt that it was one of my finest designs an attitude shared by my wife and staff. When the design was returned with comment about 'dull' color, we tried many different combinations with lead in our hearts as none were as good as the original. People have come and gone and have seen the original and the more 'colorful' attempts and all think the first is far the best. I hate to sound smug, but when I think of the people on your office staff that you might have shown the design to compared to the people that have commented favorably at this end, I am pretty sure that this end is a little heavier.[62]

In the end, Laughlin capitulated, though he seemed hesitant to give in to Lustig on purely aesthetic grounds: "We have finally gone back to your original colors. I still don't like that brown very much, but I agree with you that it is probably preferable to the livelier color, especially as the livelier design which you sent seems to be a four color job, which would be beyond our means under the circumstances."[63] Perhaps the most interesting outcome of their debate over Pound's *Selected Poems* is Lustig's next Pound cover, *ABC of Reading*. Not only did he incorporate a dazzling palette of hot pink and bright yellow, but Lustig moved even further from the associative symbols of other New Classics covers.

62 Lustig to Laughlin, February 8, 1949.

63 Laughlin to Lustig, February 13, 1949.

64 Ibid.

Instead, he came up with a composition free of both images and abstract shapes, a design that foreshadows his later, more strictly typography-based covers.

As constructive and conciliatory as Lustig and Laughlin could be, their true friendship is revealed in letters where they playfully deride one another. At one point, Laughlin lightheartedly mocked Lustig's steadfast seriousness of purpose, reporting,

> Our Psychiatric Division was considerably taken aback by the strictures which you expressed so forcibly. After due consideration, I have been instructed to pass onto you the following statement: "Alvin does not have any sense of humor. Also, he is sort of prissy. Nevertheless, he is a genius, and so we must forgive him his shortcomings." As you know, I would never think of questioning any decision reached by our Psychiatric Division. Nevertheless, I will say that in this instance, I did allow myself to express the meek rejoinder that occasionally I had known you to crack a smile.[64]

Lustig could dish it out as well, sending the notoriously tightfisted Laughlin an invoice that included line items such as:

Nervous energy consumed in warding off your suggestions calculated to lead to immoral conduct	$75
Being awakened at 2 in the morning	12
Tuition and general design instruction including use of equipment	85
Sitting with you in complete silence at the dining table while you read your mail [65]	750

65 Lustig to Laughlin, n.d. [ca. 1940–41].

William Faulkner
Light in August
New Directions
1947

A Rather New Approach

While Lustig obviously could muster up some good humor, he never left his seriousness of purpose far behind. He asserted that the designer must "be constantly on guard, cleansing his mind of the tendency to relax into a routine format, ready to experiment, play, change and alter forms."[66] An opportunity for Lustig to expand beyond his experimentation with the abstracted symbols of the New Classics series came with the inauguration of New Directions' Modern Reader series. In the mid 1940s, Laughlin distinguished the Modern Reader series by giving its books a higher price ($3.50) than what was being charged for books in the New Classics series ($1.50–1.75). He explained that Modern Readers were too big (8½" x 5⅝") to sell at a lower price, and that the demand for them was not likely going to be great enough to support the New Classics' larger print runs.[67]

In his covers for the Modern Reader series, Lustig wanted to create a new graphic vocabulary that would set it apart. Writing to Laughlin, he assessed the approach to the jackets of the New Classics series which all "grow naturally with enough potential for continuous change and development, withal maintaining continuity."[68]

66 Lustig, "What is a Designer?"
   Type Talks, May/June 1954, 6.

67 "The Modern Reader Series,"
   in Italo Zvevo, *The Confessions of Zeno*
   (New York: New Directions, 1946),
   back of dust jacket.

68 Lustig to Laughlin, n.d. [ca. 1946].

Louis-Ferdinand Celine
Journey to the End of the Night
New Directions
1949

The New Classics, which Lustig admitted had done more for his reputation than any other work, still had potential for growth and experimentation, yet he explained to Laughlin that he had in mind "a rather new approach" [69] for the Modern Reader series. Lustig relayed,

> I have just about come to the conclusion that I would like to do them all by photographic means. Using all kinds of methods, solarization, photograms, reticulation, negative melting, debossing, montage[,] I would create a set of vital images and symbols for each book. A certain number of drawn elements would also be used. Although much would be done with accidentals[,] they would be combined in a very controlled manner that would have a shock effect… They would always be arranged as abstract forms against the background of the paper and would not be half-tones covering the entire area. Nothing very good has been done in this field yet and this seems like a remarkable opportunity.[70]

While always seeking to push the form and meaning of his designs further, Lustig could also play the pragmatist:

> The tendency in book-jacket design is toward a riot of color anyway and we thought that one color designs could be quite sufficient for photographic jackets. This way you would save on one plate and one run, even though the one plate would be more expensive than one line cut. This way you could afford to give us the flat fee of $125… I do not wish to work on a basis of my fee being whatever is left from production costs.[71]

69 Lustig to Laughlin, n.d. [ca. 1946].

70 Ibid.

71 Lustig to Laughlin, n.d. [ca. 1946].

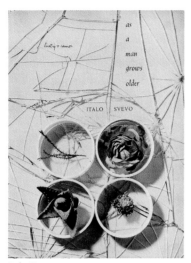

Italo Svevo
As a Man Grows Older
New Directions
1949

72 Elaine Lustig Cohen, discussion, June 12, 2008.

73 Lustig, "Graphic Design," n.p. Lustig noted the influence of the Organic Design in Home Furnishings competition organized by the Museum of Modern Art in 1940–41. He also acknowledged the influence of "the sharp, clean forms of a crisp geometry that characterize modern architecture and some modern paintings… the vitality of primitive art… technology, the electron microscope, aerial photography, the delicate tracery of steel in tension… the irrational and accidental," and "the symbolic and psychological overtones… of a group of experimental painters." (Lustig, "Modern Printed Fabrics," *Design* [1948], 27).

The Modern Reader system could break ground in book cover design *and* leave Laughlin enough in his budget to help Lustig make ends meet.

For the Modern Reader Series, Lustig chose an approach that integrated type, geometric forms and photographic elements. The photographs were often produced with the experimental techniques Lustig described, testifying to his interest in the exploration of photography in art and design by acquaintances such as Man Ray and Herbert Matter.[72] In addition to photography's place in the world of art and design, Lustig was intrigued by scientific applications of the medium. Indeed, Lustig felt that a modern design language should draw from a vast array of visual material available in contemporary life, and he was dedicated to the idea that this language could enable design to function in a socially constructive way that fine art could not. As he formulated his ideas for a seminar he taught at the 1945 Black Mountain College Summer Institute, Lustig considered not only the incorporation of visual language adopted and adapted from the realm of fine art, but also the "new visual frontiers opened up by science, the electron microscope, stroboscopic and x-ray photography."[73]

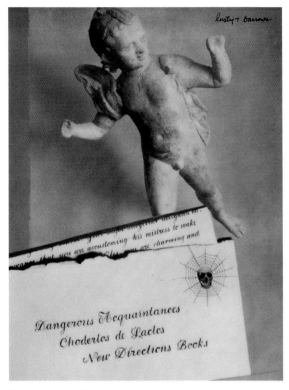

Pierre Ambroise Choderlos de Laclos
Dangerous Acquaintances
New Directions
1952

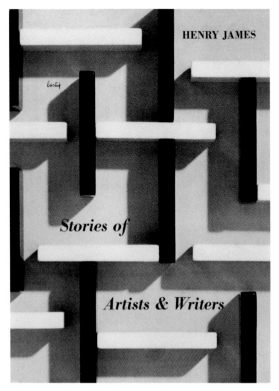

Henry James
Stories of Writers and Artists
New Directions
1956

74 Lustig to Laughlin, n.d. [ca. 1947].

Lustig's techniques for the Modern Readers' photographic covers varied from fairly straightforward integrations of individual photographs with type, to more complex montages of photographic images and lettering, to photographs of three-dimensional objects that Lustig himself constructed. In every case, Lustig's primary intention for the covers echoed that of his work for the New Classics: to make subtle, evocative allusions to the text without being simply illustrative. He hoped his covers would be suggestive, tying in to the texts in what he intended to be "an unobvious way."[74] With its beautifully balanced matrix of photographs and integration of lettering into the photographs themselves, Lustig's cover for Lorca's *Three Tragedies* weaves together seemingly disparate elements into a cohesive whole while at the same time alluding to themes in the text. By building relationships through oppositions of tone, texture, and contour, Lustig shaped visual and conceptual connections in a cover that stands as one of the most influential of his career.

Federico Garcia Lorca
Three Tragedies
New Directions
ca. 1949

Sometimes Lustig produced the photographic images for the Modern Reader jackets himself, as he did with Tennessee Williams's 27 *Wagons Full of Cotton*, and other times he partnered with well-respected experimental photographers such as George Barrows and Edward Quigley, as well as Jay Connor and Thomas Yee.[75] He saw the photograph as a way to create abstracted symbols that related to the texts of the books, often excitedly explaining his concepts to Laughlin as he formulated the images. For the earliest in the series, Italo Svevo's *The Confessions of Zeno*, Lustig relayed his initial ideas:

> I would like to photograph the back of a man's head and let it be the dominant form on the jacket. Interlocking within it would be for instance a few cigarette butts, symbols of the father, of the wife of the business partnership. Overprinting the whole thing in another color, would be some strange swirling forms to suggest madness. That sounds crude I know but it could be quite wonderful."[76]

By the time the jacket found its final, more refined form, the back of the head became a face (Lustig's own image) obscured by a charred-looking crazing that takes the place of the swirling overlay Lustig originally had planned.

75 George Barrows was a student of Ansel Adams and a friend of Robert Frank and Louis Faurer. He made photographs of Mexican masks for Ray Bradbury's *Dark Carnival* (Sauk City, Wisconsin: Arkham House, 1947), and became a photographer for the Museum of Modern Art. Edward Quigley was a Philadelphia photographer who had, by the 1940s, established himself as a successful commercial photographer and innovative art photographer with his abstractions of light. Jay Connor also photographed Lustig's architectural projects, such as the Beverly Landau apartments in Los Angeles. At one point in the late 1940s, Lustig hoped to work with James A. Fitzsimmons, a 1948 Guggenheim fellow in photography, but the partnership never seems to have materialized. (Lustig to Laughlin, n.d. [ca. 1948–49]).

76 Lustig to Laughlin, n.d. [ca. 1946]. For *As a Man Grows Older*, another Svevo work in the series, Lustig used a photograph of plant forms placed in a grid of cylinders to "symbolize the main characters. The top two are the 'hero' and Angilono. The bottom two… are the artist friend and the hero's sister." (Lustig to Laughlin, n.d. [late 1948].) "The symbols will be obscure before reading the book," Lustig explained, "but not after." (Lustig to Laughlin, December 17, 1948).

Italo Svevo
The Confessions of Zeno
New Directions
1947

Tennessee Williams
*27 Wagons Full of Cotton
and Other One-Act Plays*
New Directions
1949

Stendhal [Marie-Henri Beyle]
*Lucien Leuwen,
Book One: The Green Huntsman*
New Directions
1950

Stendhal [Marie-Henri Beyle]
*Lucien Leuwen,
Book Two: The Telegraph*
New Directions
1950

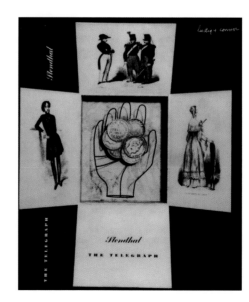

77 Lustig to Laughlin, December 5, 1948.

78 Ibid., December 17, 1948.

79 Ibid., February 26, 1950.

Unlike the design for the cover of *The Confessions of Zeno*, which evolved as the concept was realized, Lustig's vision for *27 Wagons Full of Cotton* seems to have been clear from the start. He wrote to Laughlin,

> I have an idea for *27 Wagons*, that does not describe very well, but would have great impact visually. I would get a background of an old board fence where the wood was very weatherbeaten and decayed and on to it we would nail a flower preferably a magnolia and from its wounds the equivalent of human blood would seem to drip and stain the fence. Sounds rather lurid but I think it would carry the meaning of the book and I know it could be striking visually.[77]

Within two weeks Lustig reported having successfully shot the image for the cover, adding, "We were in luck as this is just the moment that magnolias bloom."[78]

This process of building a three-dimensional construction and then photographing it was an integral part of many of the Modern Reader covers. Writing to Laughlin about the device he planned to use for Stendhal's *Green Huntsman*, and would use again for Stendhal's *The Telegraph*, Lustig revealed a process where he would sketch the idea, then build the three-dimensional maquette, using a box-like construction, photostats of old engravings, and objects that made oblique references to the tenor of the text. Then he would photograph the object in collaboration with Jay Connor.[79]

80 Imrie, "Alvin Lustig, A Versatile Designer," 60.

81 Elaine Lustig Cohen, in Aaron Britt, "A Lustig for Life," *Dwell*, December/ January 2007, 132.

82 Laughlin to Lustig, April 17, 1950.

83 Lustig to Laughlin, May 22, 1950.

The photography-based work of the Modern Reader series made its mark—by 1952, Lustig was recognized as one of the more successful American designers "who have used modern photographic techniques to advantage."[80] In retrospect, Elaine Lustig Cohen sees the Modern Reader series, with its photographic elements, as Lustig's most important work: "No one was putting it together that way. They have a rhythm, even when they're geometric, and all of them are very evocative of the text."[81]

An Untouched and Fertile Field

Just as the Modern Reader series reflected a trajectory distinct from the New Classics series, Lustig and Laughlin's collaborations would lead Lustig's cover designs in other unique directions as well. As it had with the Pound covers, mundane commercial design demands and the resultant good-natured mutual antagonism inspired innovative reconsiderations of Lustig's style. In 1950, referring to a Tennessee Williams cover, Laughlin implored Lustig, "Do try to get the title large enough so that one can read it without field glasses. That is still the general complaint that I get from the stores about your work. Things are beautiful, but people can't see the titles when they look in the windows of the stores."[82] A few weeks later, Lustig replied, "You will be happy to know that I am just ready to enter a new phase in my creative activity known as the LARGE TYPE PERIOD, and from here on I'm going to build the designs around the type, rather than vice versa. This should make everyone happy."[83] Despite their flippant exchange, Lustig's self-proclaimed "large type period" was much more than a response to discontented booksellers. It was a progression that reflected his continual rethinking of design and the interrelationship of formal and communicative issues.

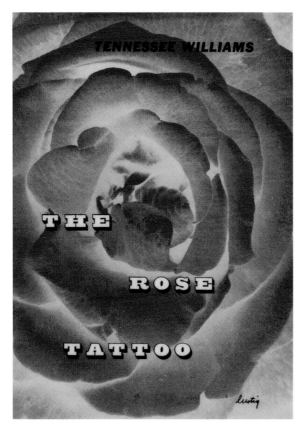

Tennessee Williams
The Rose Tattoo
New Directions
1951

Tennessee Williams
Cat on a Hot Tin Roof
New Directions
1955

For much of the New Classics series, typography had been used as a supporting element in image-dominated compositions. Nonetheless, a few covers from the series, such as *The Great Gatsby* and *ABC of Reading*, had begun to suggest the typographic experimentation that emerged to dominate Lustig's later career. Even as early as 1946, Lustig had been self-consciously rethinking the role of traditional typography, considering turning type into image as a means of creating a new graphic language for book covers. Having firmly established the aesthetic of the New Classics series and having conceived of a photographic approach for the Modern Reader series, Lustig asked Laughlin, "Why not for books that do not fall into these two series, develop an entirely abstract approach, using just lettering and shapes to evoke the spirit of the book, but avoid symbols as such?… There is an untouched and fertile field in this approach."[84]

Ronald Firbank
5 Novels by Ronald Firbank
New Directions
1949

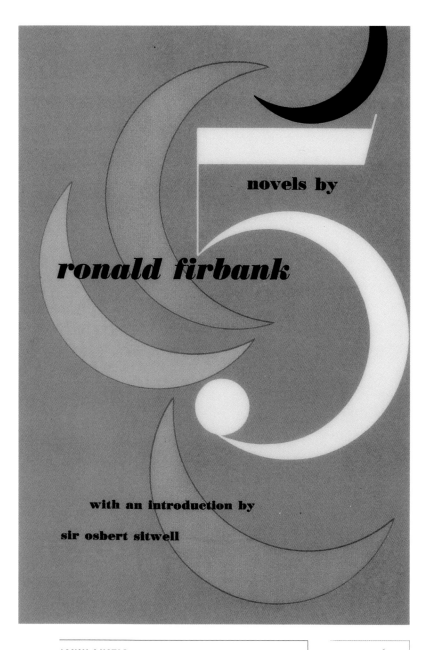

James Laughlin, ed.
*ND 12: New Directions
in Prose and Poetry*
New Directions
1950

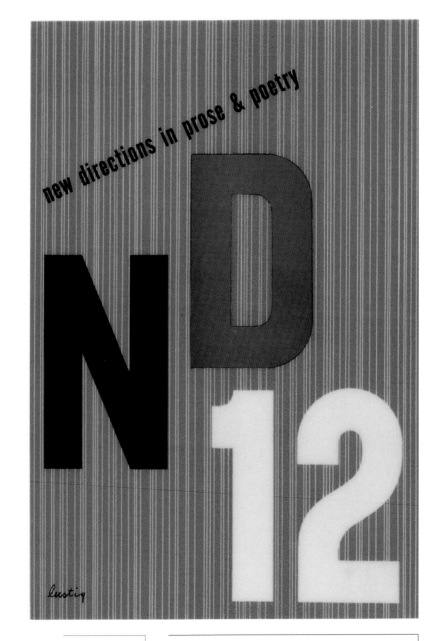

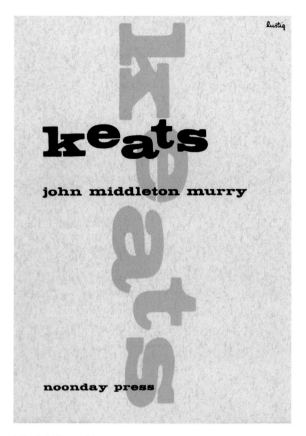

John Middleton Murry
Keats
Noonday Press
1953

Willa Cather, *Five Stories*
"Vintage Book Cover"
© 1954 by Vintage Books,
a division of Random House, Inc.
Used by permission of Alfred A. Knopf,
a division of Random House, Inc.

Andrew Carnduff Ritchie, ed.
Cover of the Museum of Modern Art
exhibition catalogue "The New Decade:
22 European Painters and Sculptors."
© 1955 The Museum of Modern Art,
New York.

In a self-conscious distillation of his repertoire of design elements, Lustig began to incorporate type as a concrete design element in and of itself, shunning the suggestive imagery of the New Classics series or the evocative photographs of the Modern Reader series. Type and color became his primary tools, and a functional, practical approach was used in an attempt to communicate the essence of the book. Lustig implemented this type-driven approach not only in his work for New Directions, but also, even more forcefully, in covers he did in the 1950s for Knopf's Vintage Books, Noonday's Meridian Books imprint, and projects such as his cover for the Museum of Modern Art's exhibition catalog *The New Decade: 22 European Painters and Sculptors.* Working on *The New Decade* with one typeface in many variations, Lustig created a perfectly balanced asymmetrical composition. He adhered to a disciplined grid structure, counterbalancing large blue text with smaller, cantilevered blue text on the right. Lustig set the artists' names in yellow-orange capital letters that flowed vertically from the top of the page and were anchored by the large "22" on the bottom left. Lustig's typographic groupings, with their intertwined elements, push and pull the viewer throughout the composition, and his complimentary colors reinforce the typographic hierarchy, creating a subtle sense of depth in the two-dimensional field.

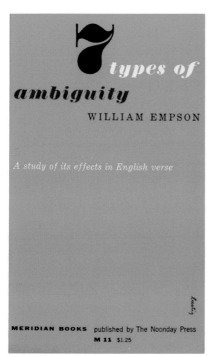

William Empson
7 Types of Ambiguity
Meridian Books
1955

In the Meridian cover for William Empson's book of literary criticism, *7 Types of Ambiguity,* Lustig played various typographic elements off the one large, key number. In his purposely top-heavy composition, the size of the type grew smaller from top to bottom, creating a cascading spatial relationship. In Lustig's hands, the type itself became the physical manifestation of the uncertainty suggested by the title. The stenciled type on Lustig's cover for Herbert Read's *Philosophy of Modern Art*, with its rhythm of alternating yellow and white components, gave a sense of aestheticized utility. Reflecting Read's theories, and his own, Lustig's stenciled type, combined with the cover, evoked a role art that could be at once refined, accessible, and serve society. Playing on ideas of class distinction in Joseph Schumpeter's essays *Imperialism* and *Social Classes*, Lustig set "Social Classes" in a decorative white script that contrasted with the imposing, all-capital, black, san-serif "Imperialism." The field of purple invited associations with royalty, while the position and color of the "2" suggested an imperial crown and helped to identify the text as two distinct essays. These typographic covers, with their subtle mixtures of typefaces on colored or patterned backgrounds, are simplified but not simplistic, bold but not stark, refined but not sterile. His idiosyncratic amalgams of different typefaces defied a pure modernist idiom and foreshadowed the eclectic use of historical styles in American design of the 1960s and the postmodernist pastiche of the 1980s.

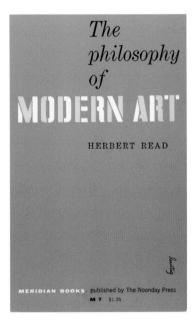

Herbert Read
The Philosophy of Modern Art
Meridian Books
1955

Thinking about his body of work in 1954, the always-reflective Lustig outlined the phases of his investigations of graphic design: from his Wright-inspired decorative type compositions, to the art-inspired abstract symbols of the New Classics covers, to his latest almost exclusively typographic work. He explained,

> In my earlier work, I was influenced primarily by more rigid architectural ideas, then around the early forties went through a phase in which the most experimental painters of either abstract-expressive or purely abstract affected me. For the last few years I have been attempting to forge in both my graphic and three dimensional problems, work that is more personal in character but which nevertheless employs more impersonal means to achieve it, and which no longer reflects the obvious derivations from modern painting which have become so apparent in the last few years. My interest in painting at the moment is not as great, as I feel it is in a state of crisis and that perhaps the creative initiative is in the process of passing to the designer, if he becomes mature enough to grasp it.[85]

Not only did he present this later work as less derivative of art, he seemed to be less concerned with reconciling art and design late in his career. To Lustig, design had come into its own.

85 Forbes, "Alvin Lustig: Design," 71.

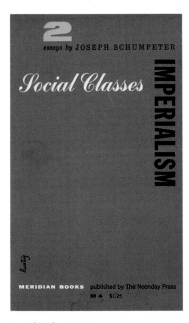

Joseph Schumpeter
Imperialism and Social Classes: 2 Essays
Meridian Books
1955

86 Lustig, "Contemporary Book Design," 2–6.

87 Lustig, "Personal Notes on Design," 18.

88 Not only did Lustig own Tschichold's books, but he also had a variety of European type books that informed his exploration of type as a design element. (Elaine Lustig Cohen, discussion, June 12, 2008; Arthur Cohen, "Alvin Lustig Remembered.")

A Peculiarly European Performance

Lustig credited the designers of the Bauhaus, as well as Ladislav Sutnar and Jan Tschichold, with setting the stage for contemporary book design and typographical innovation.[86] As he explored typographic solutions to his own design problems, Lustig seems to have been particularly struck by Tschichold's writings on typography, especially his reconsideration of the rigid modernist dogma of his own 1928 *Die Neue Typographie*. While *Die Neue Typographie* had espoused sans serif types with asymmetrical grid-like layouts, by the early 1930s, Tschichold had broadened his typographic repertoire to include a more eclectic mix of modern and traditional typefaces. Lustig's reactions to Tschichold are at once puzzling and revealing. On the one hand, Lustig condemned Tschichold for renouncing his convictions: "Tschichold, after evolving some of the basic tenets of modern typography, has decided that he is all wrong and has reverted to a kind of static conservatism that outdoes the traditionalists. We will not go into the psychology of the turncoat, but it is sufficient to say that the mentality capable of this kind of action certainly is not an example of the deeply-felt inner necessity" of heartfelt design.[87] On the other hand, Lustig was clearly impressed by Tschichold's later, more eclectic approach to typography. In addition to *Die Neue Typographie*, Lustig owned a copy of Tschichold's 1935 *Typographische Gestaltung*, and many who knew Lustig recalled how much influence Tschichold had had upon him.[88] One need only turn to the title page of *Typographische Gestaltung* to see the affinity of Lustig's late typographic covers and Tschichold's blending of typefaces.

89 Lustig, "Personal Notes on Design," 18.

90 Ibid., 17.

91 Ibid., 18–19.

Considering his own career, Lustig identified an "organic development" that might be likened to Tschichold's reassessment of typographic form. In his own work, Lustig perceived a move toward a search for a "truly organic solution, rather than the preconceived one or the never-done-before one."[89] And he, like Tschichold, concluded that rigid modernist dogma and an all-out rejection of the past offered less promise than a broader approach that would reevaluate tradition within a contemporary context. "As I have grown older," Lustig reflected, "I have found that the forms that relate to the vitality of the present turn out most often to be the greater treasures of the past."[90] And he concluded that, "as we become more mature we will learn to master the interplay between the past and the present and not be so self-conscious of our rejection or acceptance of tradition. We will not make the mistake that both rigid modernists and conservatives make, of confusing the quality of form with the specific forms themselves."[91] In his late typographic covers, Lustig seems committed to this exploration of the "quality of form" through type itself.

The fact that Lustig would share such an affinity with Tschichold's use of typography but find fault in his character begins to suggest a tension in Lustig's attitudes toward Europe and European design. He identified Tschichold's reappraisal of modernism as "a peculiarly European performance, a direct outgrowth of the manifesto-spawning character on many European art activities. It is inconceivable that a personality like Frank Lloyd Wright would suddenly announce that he had been all wrong and henceforth would build only in the classic style!"[92] It seems doubly ironic that Lustig would invoke Wright, whom he certainly respected but had found stiflingly rigid, while at the same time belittling the European movements that seem to have been the antecedents to his views on social utility and multidisciplinary design. As much as Lustig wrote about design, he only occasionally referred to European sources as precursors to his stylistic approaches and theories.[93] Still, facets of Lustig's oeuvre suggest an adaptation of earlier European movements to his own graphic vision. His experiments with type exhibit balance, hierarchy and composition that recall the functional typography of Tschichold and Ladislav Sutnar. At the same time, one can find in Lustig's work an inherent playfulness and dynamism that is reminiscent of Dadaist, Futurist and Bauhaus typographic compositions.

92 Lustig, "Personal Notes on Design," 18.

93 Lustig praised the English publications *The Architectural Review* and *Art & Industry*, and he was said to have been impressed by *Typographica*, which became available in the 1950s. (Lustig, "The Architectural Review: A Lesson in Typographic Vigor," in *Collected Writings*, 52–60, repr. from *AIGA Journal 5*, nos. 1–2, 1954, 33–39; Lustig, "Suggestions for the Development of a Quarterly Periodical," in *Collected Writings*, 61–63; Elaine Lustig Cohen and Arthur Cohen, "Alvin Lustig Remembered.") However, Lustig seemed to have a genuine distaste for Europe. For instance, he reported somewhat gleefully to Laughlin that Paul Rand went to Europe "last year and hated it thoroly [sic] coming back way ahead of schedule. It is nice to know that not everyone thinks I am crazy about the potentials of the area." (Lustig to Laughlin, May 9, 1948).

A Very Good Adjustment to the Situation

From childhood, Lustig lived with diabetes, and in the early 1950s its effects on him worsened. His vision began to fail, and by the end of 1954 he had lost sight in his right eye and then his left. While loss of sight would seem to be a devastating and insurmountable challenge, Lustig persevered and found ways to realize his graphic vision, even without sight. In 1955 Lustig wrote to Frank Malina, a rocket scientist, kinetic and light artist, and founder of the journal *Leonardo*: "I think I can say with complete modesty that we have made a very good adjustment to the situation, much of the credit of course going to the confidence and help of friends and clients… For awhile we toyed with the idea of a kind of semi-retirement in Mexico, but the continued flow of new and challenging work made us give up all ideas of retrenchement."[94] Realizing that he would have to convince his clients that he was still fully capable of meeting their needs, Lustig met the professional challenges of his blindness head on. Arthur Cohen recalled, "Elaine and Alvin gave an astonishing cocktail party to announce that Alvin was blind. All of his clients came, Philip Johnson from the Seagram's project, George Nelson, the whole design community in New York was there, and Alvin realized that he could continue."[95] Lustig not only continued to work with New Directions, Meridian and other publishers, he also continued to collaborate on various aspects of graphic design with several major architects.

94 Lustig to Frank Malina, June 1, 1955,
   Elaine Lustig Cohen Papers,
   Smithsonian Archives of American Art.

95 Arthur Cohen, "Alvin Lustig Remembered."

96 Lustig to Dr. D. Rothrook, November 17, 1955,
   in Clouse and Jules, *Alvin Lustig,
   American Modernist*, 21.

97 Arthur Cohen, "Alvin Lustig Remembered."

As late as November 1955, he reported to his doctor, "We are working on such long range accounts as signs for the General Motors Technical Center of Eero Saarinen, architectural lettering and promotional consulting for the new Seagram building by Ludwig Mies van der Rohe, and graphic and architectural lettering for the new Mondawmin shopping center in Baltimore."[96] Not only was his business running respectably despite his blindness, but Lustig was also celebrated in an exhibition at the Museum of Modern Art which opened in October 1955, showing his work with that of Italian designer Bruno Munari.

Lustig's ability to practice design without sight was testimony to the deeply thoughtful process of design he had honed over the course of his career. While he relied on his wife Elaine and assistants to bring the concept to fruition, he was able to fully visualize his designs and describe them in great detail, giving exact type specifications and referring to colors he knew from paintings and pieces of furniture in his home. "He realized," recalled Arthur Cohen, "that he could interpret accurately what his intention was, that he had developed with Elaine… and people in the office, a capacity of translation. And I think the thing that is astonishing, and that I don't think you stressed enough–his ability to describe verbally what was involved in a visual problem was astonishing."[97] This process was especially effective with Lustig's type-driven designs, for which he could refer to typefaces and colors he had committed to memory.

Ivan Chermayeff, who worked with the Lustigs as a young designer in 1955, recollected,

> For some time he could scan a book cover… from top to bottom describing his inner vision and translating his vision into typographic specifications. The results, taken down by one of his three assistants, were then given specific colors at the end. As Alvin was completely blind, we interpreted and listened and as best we could, transcribed his wishes without interference and completed the work for publication…The process, while it lasted, proved to me that taste, intelligence, and understanding of style and the priorities and meaning of content is just as important as sight. In other words, design is not just a visual profession.[98]

Lustig's diabetes continued to worsen, and he succumbed to the disease on December 5, 1955, at the age of 40. As intrepid as his adaptations to his failing health had been, Elaine Lustig Cohen speculated, "I don't think he could have continued that intensity for very long. I am sure he would have gotten discouraged: it was only a year, and he was very stubborn, and it worked, but it couldn't probably have gone on beyond that, because he would have lost touch with what was happening in the world."[99] Indeed, isolation would probably have been agonizing to a designer so dedicated to changing the world through design.

98 Ivan Chermayeff to the authors, September 6, 2007.

99 Elaine Lustig Cohen, "Alvin Lustig Remembered."

100 Chip Kidd, quoted in *Britt*,
    "A Lustig for Life," 130–31.

101 For a cursory discussion of Lustig as an
    educator, see Melson, "Alvin Lustig:
    The Designer and Teacher," *Print*, January/
    February 1969, 65–68, 110. See also
    R. Roger Remington and Barbara Hodik,
    "Alvin Lustig," in *Nine Pioneers in American
    Graphic Design* (Cambridge, Massachusetts:
    Massachusetts Institute of Technology Press,
    1989), 120–35.

Look Magazine Offices
New York, NY 1944–1945
Photograph by Maya Deren

A Forum for Expressing Ideas
Concerning the Relation of Art and Life

As tragic as Lustig's untimely death was, he made an indelible mark on the American design world. His designs still resonate, a half century after his death. Chip Kidd, one of the best known of today's American graphic designers, marveled, "His work has aged so well. Fifty-some years on it still looks fresh."[100] But beyond his work itself, Lustig made a striking impact on design theory and education through his writing and through his integral role in establishing rigorous and conceptual design programs in America.[101] As he matured, Lustig became more self-reflective and self-analytical, a tendency that fueled his desire to be an author and educator.

From the early 1940s until the last years of his life, Lustig wrote dedicatedly about design, publishing many articles about his design process and philosophy in a variety of design journals. Yet he strove for more, and looked to Laughlin as a possible vehicle for publishing these specialized design projects. In 1946, he pitched a pamphlet series, asking the ever-thrifty Laughlin, "Would you be interested in starting an inexpensive pamphlet series to sell at about 75 cents on the problems of design? It would not necessarily deal with only one personality but be a forum for expressing ideas concerning the relation of art and life. At the moment there is nothing that does this specifically."[102] The pamphlet series never materialized, but Lustig and Laughlin each wrote short pieces for a book about Lustig's covers for New Directions, published by the Gotham Book Mart Press in 1947.[103] In 1948, Lustig pitched a more substantial book on his own work to Laughlin:

> An increasing number of people have asked me when I am going to put out a book of my work, which is beginning to reach sufficient volume and variety to think about such a project. Would such a book interest you? You have offered to publish anything I wanted to write but I feel verbal statements coming from me are pointless, or if I make them, they should be in connection with examples of my work... Also I think I could marshal a fairly impressive group of personalities to make statements to incorporate with the material if we wanted them.[104]

102 Lustig to Laughlin, March 25, 1946.

103 Laughlin and Lustig, *Bookjackets by Alvin Lustig.*

104 Lustig to Laughlin, April 15, 1948.

105 Lustig to Harry Ford (proposal);
   Sidney R. Jacobs to Alvin Lustig, July 28, 1955;
   Ford to Lustig, October 24, 1955,
   Graphic Design Archive, RIT.

Lustig's project was never accomplished through Laughlin, but he continued to pursue the idea of a book on his activities in design into the last year of his life. In a proposal submitted to Harry Ford at Alfred A. Knopf, Lustig outlined chapters addressing practical design principles such as order, structure, typography, and architectural lettering. Other chapter titles that he proposed echoed his philosophical concerns as a designer: "The Designer in a Living Society," "Private and Public Symbols," and "Design Education." The editors at Knopf seem to have seriously considered the project, but ultimately, in October 1955, they wrote to Lustig explaining that they did not feel they could publish the book to Lustig's standards.[105] It was not until after Lustig's death that a substantial book of his writing on design philosophy finally appeared. In 1958, former Lustig student Holland R. Melson edited and published *The Collected Writings of Alvin Lustig*, a selection of both previously published and never-before-published essays. The book was indeed substantial, but it lacked the coherence that Lustig himself had imagined for the book he had hoped to publish. While Lustig never saw his writing achieve the high profile visibility that he had envisioned, his essays were among the most thoughtful and complex of his era in America.

Lustig's professional drive and high ethical standards pushed him throughout his career, and his engagement with the theoretical and practical aspects of his field intensified year by year. His career was punctuated by outstanding successes and remarkable achievements, yet it was not without its frustrations, as his thwarted attempts to publish a book on design attest. Lustig had grand notions of the role of the designer as a multifaceted practitioner who could change the world, but he had to deal with the realities of life as a designer.

While he seemed to prefer living in California, he was drawn to New York for professional opportunities, first to work for *Look* magazine in the mid 1940s and again at the end of the decade. The second New York sojourn, which would last until the end of his life, seems to have been fueled, initially at least, by necessity. Having trouble collecting enough fees from clients and not getting as many jobs outside of graphic design as he would like, Lustig wrote to Laughlin from Los Angeles in 1949 that

> My paradise looks more and more tarnished.
> I am beginning to wonder seriously if perhaps I should come back to NY… As long as I was getting building done I did not mind as that was what I had come for, but building has become very quiet the last few months and I find myself doing mostly graphic design. If I am doing only graphic work I certainly belong back in NY, on the other hand I don't want to do just graphic work so should I be patient and so on…?"[106]

106 Lustig to Laughlin, May 5, 1949.

107 Lustig to Laughlin, February 26, 1950.

108 Lustig to Laughlin, n.d.

Slightly less than a year later, he relayed to Laughlin his need in Los Angeles for "at least one solid arrangement that would assure us the means for basic living and upon which we could slowly build a wider practice."[107] The idea of a return to New York seemed to be a professional defeat to Lustig, who wrote to Laughlin, "For me returning to the city would be a retreat. It has never been my policy to do things in which I did not believe, no matter what advantage might incur."[108] Lustig returned to New York, and as much as this might have seemed a defeat at first, he found ways to excel on the East Coast. In the 1950s he not only continued to deepen his investigations into design theory and practice, but his role as an educator truly began to blossom.

Lustig was indeed able to make an indisputable impact with his ideas in the classroom. For Lustig, a key factor in the realization of a broadly conceived and conceptually rigorous design practice lay in the creation of new approaches to the education of designers. As a mature designer, Lustig put great effort into devising new methods of educating designers. In 1945 he taught a summer seminar at Black Mountain College in North Carolina, an experience that established new friendships and strengthened old ones in the fields of art and design. It also offered him the opportunity to articulate his design philosophy and pass it on to new generations of designers. Not only did he bring his astute contemplations of the role of the designer to the classroom, he also published his ideas in a special issue of the journal *Design* that was devoted to Black Mountain College.[109] In the late 1940s and 1950, Lustig also taught at West Coast institutions such as the Art Center School in Los Angeles and the University of Southern California.

By the 1950s as he settled back in New York, Lustig was not simply teaching, he was helping to formulate entire design programs. Lustig saw a great failure in the design education of his day, where typical design curricula took a trade school approach that exhibited "the ability to produce highly specialized technicians—but the inability to produce people related in understanding to a larger social community or human endeavor."[110] Yet he saw equally dismal failures in the more academic settings of the University, where he found "people who talked quite cleverly about almost everything and with highly developed critical faculties, but who couldn't do a thing."[111] The solution, for Lustig, was an integration of theory and practice, where technique would be informed by the conceptual, where the visions of designers could find their way into real-world applications.

109 Lustig, "Graphic Design," n.p.

110 Lustig, "Designing, a Process of Teaching," 33–46.

111 Ibid.

112 Lustig to Laughlin, April 12, 1945;
     Lustig, "Design Program for the University
     of Georgia," in *Collected Writings*, 28.

In 1951, Josef Albers, who had recruited Lustig to
Black Mountain College, recommended him to help develop
the design program at the University of Georgia. As he
conceived the Georgia program, Lustig envisioned a
curriculum that produced designers conversant in a variety
of fields, creating graduates who could contribute to the
larger social role he felt was so important to design.
He hoped to form the students into what he called "design
integrators" who would be able "to unify all aspects of a problem,
technical, economic and psychological." This integration,
Lustig asserted, lent itself to an understanding of the "larger
human implications of design."[112]

Lustig in his Hollywood Office
1945 © J. Paul Getty Trust.
Used with permission. Julius Shulman
Photography Archive, Research Library
at the Getty Research Institute
(2004.R.10).

113 Rob Roy Kelly, "The Early Years of Graphic Design at Yale University," *Design Issues* 17, no. 3 (Summer 2001), 3–14. See also Philip Meggs and Alston Purvis, *Meggs' History of Graphic Design* (Hoboken, New Jersey: John Wiley and Sons, 2006), 382–83.

114 Richard DeNatale, "Alvin Lustig Remembered."

115 Kelly, "Early Years," 8.

Lustig's greatest opportunity to create designers with an integrative approach to design's technical skills, theoretical bases and social roles took place at Yale University. Josef Albers was appointed in 1950 as chair of the newly established Department of Design at Yale. Albers in turn invited Alvin Eisenman to direct the graphic design program, the first ever established at a major American university. As they looked to staff the new program, Eisenman and Albers brought Lustig in as a visiting critic in 1951.[113] Until 1954, when his health made it impossible to teach, Lustig helped lay the foundation for one of the most rigorous design programs in America. He brought to the program his fervent belief in the obligations of the designer to society.

Richard DeNatale, who studied with Lustig at Yale, recalled that Lustig was responsible for the "introduction of social problems into the curriculum, dealing with problems which needed solutions that were related to people and people's reactions to those problems."[114] In addition, many of Lustig's late-career typographic interests were reflected in the pedagogy he helped to develop at Yale. Former student Rob Roy Kelly recalled the rigor with which typography was taught in the early years at Yale: "Typography was taught as a minimal art… There was always painstaking consideration for the choice and appropriateness of type as it related to content and function. The 'color' and 'texture' of text was an important consideration… The standard for styling was to use as few type changes as possible, and to rely more on visual tension, leading, and placement."[115] The subtle interplay of form and meaning in Lustig's typographic book cover designs had been adapted into the curriculum at Yale.

Lustig's dedication as an educator led him to aspire beyond the already unprecedented depth of the Yale curriculum. He strove to extend the Yale curriculum past the boundaries of the campus, in order to reconcile the disparity between the day-to-day demands of the practicing designer and the theoretical world of academia. Lustig proposed an on-going "Experimental Workshop in Graphic Design," functioning as a collaborative partnership with the Museum of Modern Art (MoMA). The workshop would be a self-conscious interchange "between the graphic design profession and a more experimental unhampered laboratory," providing the opportunity for "proven practitioners in the field to work on projects of a sort which the usual pressure of their business would not allow."[116] Lustig himself was to serve as the director of the proposed workshop for Yale, and Mildred Constantine would be the director for MoMA. "Proven practitioners" to describe the professional participants in the workshop was an understatement. The list of designers Lustig hoped to have involved was a compendium of midcentury design masters: from Yale there was Albers, Eisenman, and Herbert Matter; from MoMA, Philip Johnson and Arthur Drexler; a consulting advisory board included Charles Coiner, Leo Lionni, Bill Golden, Charles Eames, Robert Osborn, Walter Howe, Bradbury Thompson, Alexey Brodovitch; and a less official group of international advisors included Willem Sandberg from Holland, Max Bill from Switzerland, Otl Aicher from Germany, and Bruno Munari from Italy.[117] Sadly, Lustig died before his experimental workshop could be implemented.

116 Lustig, "Experimental Workshops in Graphic Design for Yale University," in *Collected Writings*, 75.

117 Ibid., 76–77.

Though Lustig's own books on design never would be completed and his participation in the design program was discouragingly short, his contribution to American graphic design was immense. His book cover work is still held up as the epitome of progressive American design at midcentury. His immediate students and protégés, such as Chermayeff, DeNatale and Kelly, became outstanding designers and educators of their own generation. Lustig laid the groundwork for future Yale educators such as Paul Rand, who began at Yale the year after Lustig died and continued teaching there until 1993. Lustig's calls for the creation of repositories of type specimens, periodicals, graphic collections, and other information related to graphic design spawned an interest in the creation of design archives preserving the sorts of materials he found so lacking in his youth.[118]

Today, design students are introduced to Lustig's work because of the many groundbreaking ways he shaped the visual profile of the most avant-garde writers of his age, and how he infused his designs with a contemporary visual vocabulary that echoed the worlds of art and photography. Lustig's experiments with photography and typography helped to establish basic principles that shape design education today, principles such as typographic contrast, structural hierarchy, and dynamic physical and interpretive oppositions between compositional elements.

118 Lustig, "Experimental Workshops in Graphic Design for Yale University," in *Collected Writings*, 76.

Lustig's ability to pull together disparate ideas, both formally and conceptually, solidified his legacy in the world of publishing, design and design education. Whether the point in question was how to balance art and design, education and practice, personal expression and commerce, private vision and public audience, or preconceived ideas and organic discoveries, Lustig believed in directly confronting contrasting issues and directly contributing to society. Lustig created a major shift in how book covers were conceived, designed and consumed. He took full advantage of the freedom that his sympathetic and supportive client, James Laughlin, gave him. The systems Lustig created structured the publications of New Directions into distinct groups, while still allowing for each book to have its own personality, a personality that always reflected the nature of the book's content. These unique systems he created for the different New Directions series are still benchmarks in today's design world. In defining an aesthetic identity for New Directions, Lustig was able to re-conceptualize and revolutionize the design of book covers, transforming the bland protective device of the book jacket into a masterpiece of visual communication.

Portrait of Lustig
1949, Photograph by Jeff Moses

ACKNOWLEDGMENTS

The authors would like to thank our Rutgers colleagues
Ian Watson, Nick Kline, Crystal Grant and Rob Gonzalez;
our fellow Lustig scholars Elaine Lustig Cohen, Doug Clouse,
Greg D'Onofrio and Patricia Belen; our RIT collaborators
David Pankow, Molly Q. Cort, Kari Horowicz, Patricia Cost
and Bruce Ian Meader; and of course our families,
Brenda McManus, Joan Cummins, and Grace Sternberger.

ABOUT THE AUTHORS

Ned Drew teaches graphic design courses and the history of graphic design at Rutgers University-Newark. He is also the director of The Design Consortium, a student/teacher run design studio that focuses on non-profit, community-based projects.

Paul Sternberger (Ph.D.) is an Associate Professor of Art History at Rutgers University-Newark, who specializes in American Art and the History of Photography. He is the author of *Between Amateur and Aesthete: The Legitimization of Photography in America, 1880–1900* and co-author with colleague Ned Drew, *By It's Cover: Modern American Book Cover Design.* Other publications include various journal articles in *American Art*, *Photographies*, and the *Journal of the History of Collections*.

COLOPHON

Design	Bruce Ian Meader
Production	Molly Q. Cort and Marnie Soom
Typefaces	Sabon designed by Jan Tschichold and Frutiger designed by Adrian Frutiger
Paper	Blazer Silk
Printing	More Vang Alexandria, Virginia